# Cover Your Ass!

Illustrated by David Shaw

Bureaucrat X

# Cover Your Ass!

## or How to Survive in a Government Bureaucracy

Hurtig Publishers
Edmonton

Hurtig Publishers
10560 105 Street
Edmonton Alberta

ISBN: 0-88830-135-9

Printed and bound in Canada

# Contents

I am indebted to my wife, who spent many a day,
pencil poised and sharpener at the ready,
editing this work. How our relationship survived
her insistence that entire chapters be re-arranged
and my initial resistance to any change, I will
never know. In the end, I gave in. The result is
what follows.

This book is dedicated to the bureaucratic
mentality that produced the following regulation:

Regulation to Amend Regulation 383
of Revised Regulations of - - -, 1970
Made Under The - - - Act

1.(1) subclause VII of clause N of subsection *i*
of section 1 of regulation 383 of Revised
Regulations of - - -, 1970, as remade by subsection
*ii* section 1 of - - - Regulation 714/73,
is revoked.

**Introduction**

Everyone has had at least one frustrating encounter with a government official. Many of us have come to admire the job security and salary level of these bureaucrats, especially in view of their propensity for avoiding any responsibility. Although I didn't know it at the time, a major turning point in my life occurred while observing a fellow civil servant in a government office, many years ago. He was talking with an elderly couple who, from the looks of things, had something of a problem. About twenty minutes went by while the clerk listened to the protestations of these people and attempted to set them straight.

Suddenly another clerk appeared from the back room, tapped his workmate on the shoulder, and said, "Coffee break, Harry." Harry arose immediately, informed the elderly couple that this new gentleman would take care of them, and left.

"Okay, what seems to be the problem?" asked our newly arrived official; whereupon this poor couple had to go back to the beginning and start over again.

That was the birth of my fascination with government bureaucrats, and I have been studying them ever since. In the meantime I have progressed through sundry positions to become a very highly placed, lavishly paid official (government always makes its employees offers that they cannot possibly refuse, as long as they remember to cover their asses along the way). In order to gain first-hand information on bureaucrats, I have infiltrated the ranks of several provincial and federal ministries over the last thirty years, and have been carrying on my observations in a number of different departments. The events I describe herein are true, although names have been changed and departments disguised. In the course of research for this book, I have interviewed civil servants at all levels of government in every province. The events recorded here were either witnessed by me or were reported by two or more subjects – in triplicate.

In writing this book I have attempted to provide an honest account of what your civil servants do on your time. I have been motivated by three considerations. First, governments spend a great deal of *our* money every year, and yet little is known about what they really do and how they actually work. Second, governments are growing at a phenomenal rate, and an ever-increasing proportion of the workforce is employed by them. So there is a great need for a how-to book – a survival guide – for those people who don't want to risk the criticism wreaked upon labour unions, welfare recipients, multinational corporations, politicians, and teachers, but who thoroughly enjoy a career wherein they do little productive work while possibly doing some irreparable damage and cashing in on the benificent bottomless pit of the public purse. Thus this book has been specially designed with the bureaucrat and potential bureaucrat in mind: the vocabulary level is very low, the type is very large, and for those who still have comprehension problems, there are instructive illustrations that seek to transmit basic survival tactics simply and quickly.

Finally, I am motivated by the fact that if this book earns me enough money, I will be able to escape from the bureaucrats. *Please* recommend it to your friends.

Bureaucrat X
August 1977

Cover Y

ur Ass!

# 1

# Delusions of Grandeur:
# *Job Titles*
# *& Descriptions*

In dealing with a government bureaucracy either as a citizen or as a new employee, an important thing to remember is that nothing is really what it seems. This is the case with both job titles and job descriptions. Let's look at the meaning of the titles of some of the people you are likely to encounter. (The glossary at the end of the book provides definitions for the important titles and terms for your reference.)

Job titles in government perform two important functions. First, they give people an inflated feeling of self-importance by glamorizing their jobs. For instance, the next time you call a government office to get information or assistance and wind up being passed from official to official to official, stop when they tell you to talk to the Co-ordinator of Solid Pollutant Removal or the Supervisor of Recycling Technicians; you have just been passed to the head janitor.

I once had the impressive title of Project Manager and was even given business cards with this title printed on it under my name, so that I could pass them out to people. I felt very important and proud. Then I discovered that no one who worked on this project reported to me and that I had absolutely no authority. I was probably given

Four Bureaucrats in an Advanced State (Province?) of Grandiosity...

this meaningless title and business card to satisfy my complaints, since I had complained about having nothing to do.

In one department where I worked there were a number of Assistant Deputy Ministers (See Glossary), one of whom had an assistant. The assistant had a title: Assistant to the Assistant Deputy Minister. I had met this person a number of times and had been to some meetings with her, but I never could determine exactly what she did. Whatever her duties were, they were quite onerous for, in time, she hired an assistant. This new person's title was (you guessed it) Assistant to the Assistant to the Assistant Deputy Minister.

The titles used in government circles do more than just elevate people to absurdly inflated status. They also disguise political exile. The power struggles that go on in the civil service rival anything you could find anywhere – with one deviation. While a *coup d'etat* in a Latin American country will often result in deaths and political executions, our civil service is too civilized for such extremes; therein lies the origin of "civil" in our title. People are not assassinated or fired; they are given new jobs with nice titles and very few responsibilities. Take, for example, the case of a former Chief Consultant (whatever that means) who had a very impressive title (and salary) to keep him out of the way. In the re-organization (See Glossary) of his department, he was made Acting Manager until the appointment could be made official. Before the re-organization was completed and new positions were confirmed, we began to re-organize again. The person who appointed the Acting Manager was shifted to a new department and the new person in charge removed the Acting Manager. Soon he became a Special Advisor; all his duties were removed and he was given a little project to work on while drawing the same salary.

One who is considering a bureaucratic career should be very suspicious of job descriptions. These are official government documents that set out your duties, the amount of time that is to be devoted to each duty and the qualifications required for the job. When it comes to inventiveness, job descriptions far surpass any job title ever conceived in the dusty recesses of the bureaucratic mentality.

You might think that describing a job is a very simple chore. But in the government, it is not simple. A job description is a highly specialized document that must be developed by someone who is trained in the art of obscuring a simple task in a plethora of exaggerated and technical specifications - in short, bureaucratic jargon. Once the job description is prepared, it must be evaluated and the position must be classified. That is, another person who is specially trained - not in the art of *writing* these documents, but in the art of *reading* them - reads it. This person counts up key words and evaluates the complexity of the tasks. He or she then decides how the position should be classified, *e.g.* secretary, clerk, economist - depending on the rules. He also decides what level the position should be, *e.g.* Clerk 1, Clerk 2, or Clerk 3. The higher the number, the more the money.

This whole process would be much clearer if we followed the steps involved in hiring a new person.

*Step One:* Harry is a Statistician 3 and chief of a section involved in putting together and analysing numbers. He has decided that because of the increased workload he needs an assistant. Permission is granted by his boss (the director), and Harry proceeds to hire someone.

*Step Two:* Harry meets with Joe, a job-description writer, and they discuss what type of person is required. Harry asks for a professional statistician to work for him. He really needs someone to perform a simple clerical function, but Harry has been a civil servant for quite some time. He is familiar with the fact that the more people you have reporting to you, the more important you are. He also knows that the higher the pay that the people who report to you get, the more important you are (See Chapter Seven: The Joys of Empire Building). Therefore, he wants his assistant to be a statistician.

*Step Three:* Harry tells Joe what the duties of this new employee will be, and Joe translates these duties into the proper terminology required for such an official document.

*Step Four:* Joe goes back to his own department to compose the job description, which may take a couple of weeks (with luck), since Joe has many of these documents to write and he must consult the proper manuals. When finished, the description is sent to Harry for approval.

*Step Five:* After Harry has approved the description, it is sent off to the Classification Section. Harry requested a Statistician 1, so the classification people read the document carefully, checking and counting key words to verify the fact that this position really does require a Statistician 1. They decide that the duties call only for a Clerk 4, and return the document to Harry. This happens about two months after they have received it, since these people are quite busy and this is a difficult job.

*Step Six:* Harry and Joe re-think the problem, change a number of words in the document, and re-submit the modified job description. This takes another couple of weeks.

*Step Seven:* Another two months pass before the classification section returns the job description with its stamp of approval. Harry can now begin the process of hiring a statistician, only eight months after he decided that he needed more staff.

Below are a few simplified examples of the differences between the job description and the real duties some lucky person will perform.

| Job Description | Real Duties |
| --- | --- |
| The co-ordination and collection of statistical data | Copy numbers from other government publications and computer print-outs |
| The development and maintenance of an editing system to ensure that minimal standards of reliability and validity are maintained | Make sure you copied the numbers down right |
| Analysis and inter-pretation of complex social data | Calculate percentages |
| The need to deal on a professional level with various tiers of government and members of the public | Be able to tell people what you have done, should they bother to ask |

The following qualifications are needed for this job:

1. A basic understanding of computer systems and preferably some programming ability. (*Reason:* you will be copying numbers from a computer print-out.)

2. Knowledge of the available literature in the field. (*Reason:* you will have to copy numbers out of different books.)

3. A high level of oral and written communication skills. (*Reason:* someone might ask you a question.)

One of the best government job descriptions on record ran on for five pages of single-spaced type. Below are presented some of the duties written in this job description; with only the key words changed to disguise the department.

> Is responsible for the analysis and review of a comprehensive series of publications describing the incidence of haemorrhoids in Canada, and the deployment of medical staff and equipment to combat haemorrhoids and to enforce good intestinal habits. The data obtained from each agency must be analysed according to standards of reasonableness and by integrating haemorrhoid data (health disorder) with sociodemographic data (census, unemployment, divorce, education, etc.) in order to determine efficiency of the reporting agency and so that haemorrhoids as a measure of health disorder can be related itself be analysed in both annual and quarterly systems:
>
> – by analysing various methods of presentation, determining those which best describe the phenomenon of haemorrhoids, and organizing the data into appropriate formats;
>
> – by applying mathematical concepts to reported data in order to arrive at an estimate in areas of non-coverage;
>
> – by analysing current and historical data to establish trends and inter-relationships;
>
> – by writing a descriptive text and formulating accompanying charts and statements; and
>
> – by conducting a subsequent review of the final reports prior to publication and by writing press releases outlining highlights.

If you think that this is impressive, you should read the rest of the duties. This passage accounts for only 50 per cent of them. Imagine the consternation of the new employee at the sight of this document. How would anyone be able to do all of this?

# 2

# Disillusionment: Your First Days as a Bureaucrat

*A* newly hired bureaucrat begins the first day of a government job with the acquisition of an impressive title and a job description that sounds impossible to fulfil. Is it any wonder that he is filled with awe and foreboding when he reports for work? It is not long, however, before he begins to wonder what is really going on.

Some people are very naive and it takes them a while to stop taking their described duties seriously. Until they realize that the whole thing is a sham, they beat their heads against the wall insisting on honesty and integrity. No one else seems to care!

Other people learn a little faster and they are lucky. One chap, for instance, after only a year in the civil service, was chided for heading straight to the bathroom upon arrival at work and remaining there for twenty minutes. He commented that he could see no good reason why he should perform these duties on his own time when he could do them on government time. (When it was suggested that he might get a bit uncomfortable at night, he insisted that nights were no problem. However, he said, it does get a bit tricky on the weekends – and long weekends were pure agony.)

The new employee's first morning is usually

spent filling out numerous forms that will enable him to get a pay cheque and ensure that the proper deductions are removed. With luck, he might get a pay cheque in four to six weeks. In some departments he may have to swear an oath of allegiance and sign an oath of secrecy. Having accomplished all this, he is sent off to his section.

On one such occasion I arrived at my new office to begin what seemed to be a very exciting and challenging position. I had accepted the offer partly because one of the people who had interviewed me struck me as being quite bright and sincere. Certainly the organization was anxious to have me, because they wanted me to start almost immediately, even though I had to move from another city. When the organization had agreed upon my terms for a starting date and expenses, I reported for work. After the form-filling ceremony, the personnel representative informed me that I was to report to the person who would be (in industry) the equivalent of the first vice-president. The VP was heading off to a meeting and suggested that I be delivered to the next-in-command.

That fine gentleman sat opposite me in his office and stared at me in some discomfort. He was joined shortly by his assistant, whom I had met before. After exchanging the usual pleasantries, they both mumbled that they really didn't know what I could do for the organization, or what they were supposed to do with me, or where my office was to be located. After numerous embarrassed pauses and lulls in the conversation, one of the gentlemen, showing considerable thoughtfulness, told me where the bathroom was. I replied that I really wasn't ready for it yet. After a few more pauses, he suggested that I go for coffee.

After finishing my coffee and pondering the whereabouts of the impressive people who had interviewed me; I returned to the nice man's office to be told that he had been called out to a meeting. It was suggested that I use a temporarily vacant office and read a few reports. Fortunately, I was discovered later in the day by the person with whom I was to work. I had been spotted that morning by one of the people who had been at my interview and when I disappeared, a search party was sent out. This was the start of a tremendous adventure that was to see me (in a period of fifteen months) report to five different people (none of whom knew what my qualifications were or what I was supposed to do), and move to four different offices.

Often, in the recruit's first few weeks as a bureaucrat, people will give him a lot of helpful advice to see him through this trying time. His first year is probationary and, theoretically, he can be fired in that time without being given a reason. I was told early in my career to "keep my nose clean" for the first year. Then, once I was a permanent civil servant, I would be set for life and could just sit back and wait for retirement. Since I was in my mid-twenties at the time, I felt that this counsel reflected a strange attitude, even coming from a fifty-year-old. If I followed this advice, I would spend close to forty years doing as little as possible while waiting for retirement. But since that time I've discovered that many civil servants adhere to this theory and look upon their work as "pensionable time."

Such advice, however well-intentioned, was unnecessary, since it is almost impossible not to pass your probationary period. For a boss to recommend that your employment be terminated is for him to admit his own incompetence in recruiting qualified staff and his own inability to provide proper guidance and supervision. One very cynical civil servant pointed out that in order to be fired from a job in his ministry you would have to rape the Deputy Minister (a woman) on a table in the cafeteria at high noon. Even then, she would have to swear out an affidavit stating that she did not like it.

More realistic advice for the newcomer would be to try and latch onto a director who was a hustler and obviously on his way up the ladder. If he liked you and was a successful politician, his favours would fall upon you. What's more, never kick someone who is down and in political disfavour, since you never knew when this person, through a change in the bureaucratic structure, would bounce back again. Political alignments in the government are very complex and delicate structures.

Here is the story of one man's fortune. George was quite ambitious and was liked by the Deputy Minister. As a result, George was awarded numerous promotions, which made him powerful. Soon, however, the Deputy Minister left and the new deputy disliked George. Consequently, our bright star fell and, in the shuffling, he lost all his power. He continued to collect his pay cheque and bide his time. Eventually another minister, who liked him, was installed. Now the fallen star arose and again shone brightly, while the Deputy Minis-

ter sat quietly, waiting for the inevitable Cabinet shuffle or election. This would lead to the minister's replacement and leave George open for shuffling again.

By not insulting or attacking anyone you are following the CYA principle, which governs all civil servants the world over. The abbreviation CYA stands for "Cover Your Ass." No servant of the people worth his salt would dare to leave his posterior exposed, just as no self-respecting Old West gunfighter would dare to sit with his back to the saloon door! In fact, the philosophy of covering one's ass is so important that it governs every move a bureaucrat makes. No memo is finalized, no committee set up, no report released, no policy set or promotion given without the person contemplating such action considering every political ramification that this move could have. When all the eventualities are considered, the proposed action is modified to reduce the impact against one's self. The ass is covered. Rarely is advice given to the new recruit on how to do his job; almost all counsel pertains to survival in the bureaucracy – covering your ass. Most information regarding duties is so vague that one is forced to ask for work, out of boredom or embarrassment.

On your first day on the job, none of your colleagues will come right out and ask, but they will be desperately anxious to know your salary. I am not really sure why this is of such vital importance, but civil servants tend to be abnormally preoccupied with their own and everyone else's salaries. I once received a Christmas card from a former colleague who informed me on the card that "We just got a raise and I got a promotion. I'm now making X dollars a year and by next December I will be up to Y. Have a happy holiday." There are many ways of finding out a person's salary range without being so tactless as to ask. Everyone is classified in a particular category and in a numerical level within that category, as we saw in the discussion of job descriptions in the previous chapter. Thus you might be a Program Manager (PM) at the "one" level – a PM 1. People in the know can tell immediately that you earn between ten and twelve thousand dollars a year.

In a town where almost everyone works for the government, it is almost impossible to go to a party without people floating around trying to determine your income and, hence, your importance. It is particularly enjoyable to be a consultant on contract; because such a person has no definite category, people are quite frustrated by their inability to determine your salary. One hapless bureaucrat attended a conference and was chatting to a director from her own department at a cocktail party when the inevitable question of rank arose. When she told him her classification, he removed a set of cards from his pocket, shuffled through until he found the right one, decided from her salary range that she lacked enough importance to warrant his time, and wandered off to find someone more prestigious with whom to talk.

Eventually, your new colleagues will somehow manage to find out with amazing accuracy what your salary is long before you realize it. I once found myself at a meeting with my boss and colleagues that was called to stem a departmental revolt arising from the fact that I had been hired at a salary higher than their own. The fact that I had more education and experience than my colleagues did was deemed not relevant. They were upset because the hiring of someone over their heads interfered (so they thought) with their own chances of advancement. My boss very neatly shifted the blame for me and my salary onto the public service commission, which had the final say on salary. Their decision, it was pointed out to my co-workers, was based on the commission's rules concerning the level of education and the amount of work experience, and there was little our boss could do. After this meeting, my colleagues became much friendlier.

After the shock of the first few days as a bureaucrat begins to wear off, you begin noticing all sorts of fascinating events taking place around you. The following chapters describe these events and their significance in the culture of the civil servant. One of the most important ways to cover your ass, you will learn, is through careful attention to entrenchment of your position through the politics of office equipment.

# 3

# The Insignia of Rank: *Office Space & Furniture*

In the military services you can determine the importance of someone by noting the number of pieces of cloth sewn on his sleeve or on his shoulder. Someone with two V-shaped pieces of cloth on his sleeve is more important than someone with only one; those with bars on their shoulders are the most important – ranked, of course, by the number of these bars.

Civil servants do not have such clearly visible marks of importance. Some consider the briefcase or attaché case to be a mark of distinction, but even the lowliest clerk can emulate his director and transport his lunch to work in an attaché case. The briefcase does have some importance, however. In one department a new employee was chastised by the director for not taking his briefcase home with him; the new employee pointed out that it was not really necessary for him to do so, since he always bought his lunch in the cafeteria.

In some departments a significant measure of status is the time of arrival at work. The professional staff are noted for appearing about half an hour late and sauntering down the hall with a polystyrene cup of coffee in one hand and the morning paper in the other.

"I don't get paid for how much I do," one such

professional informed me, "but for how much I know." However, this attitude is not an effective indication of rank, since most civil servants like to give the impression of being overworked. With the advent of flexible hours, we never really know when someone is supposed to start and finish work.

Traditionally, the real mark of rank has always been associated with offices, their space, and their furnishings. Someone who gets an office is obviously more important than someone who does not get one and must share accommodations. Below are eight examples of how to match equipment to fit one's rank.

1. At the lowest level, a *Clerk* is given a small desk and a chair with a back but no arms. The desk, of course, is in a row of other desks with very little free space around it.

2. A *Supervisor of Clerks* gets a slightly larger desk and possibly a larger and more decorative blotter to put on it. The chair will have arm rests. The furniture will be located in such a way as to distinguish the occupant from others of lower rank. For example, it will be facing in a different direction from all the others.

3. The *Junior Executive* will get a cubicle or completely enclosed office, but it will not be very large. The desk and chair will be the same as in Stage One and Stage Two, but he will probably have his own filing cabinet and a side chair for visitors.

4. Above Stage Three (say, a *Supervisor of Junior Executives*), we get a larger office, a credenza, extra filing cabinets, and more than one side chair, since we will probably be entertaining more than one visitor.

5. By the time you reach Stage Five, you can expect a much larger desk, made either of solid wood or a richer looking wood finish, and a high-backed swivel chair. You will also have a larger credenza to supplement your filing cabinets, a coffee table and chairs for entertaining visitors, and a bookcase.

6. Your next step up the office ranking will give you three important additions to what you have accumulated in Stage Five. You now get a rug on your floor, a couch to go with the coffee table and chairs, and your very own secretary to sit outside your door.

7. As we approach the top, we get as many as six

Only 50% Coverage is not enough...

good prints on the wall; not one, but two secretaries; and a couch, chairs, and coffee table outside your office so that your visitors can sit in comfort while they wait for you.

8. Finally, at the very top of your department or branch, one of your two secretaries gets her own office. The one filing cabinet that you started with has now grown to about ten and these are stored in your senior secretary's office.

Space and furniture are so important to our bureaucrats that some individuals will add their own personal furnishings to the office in order to give the impression that they are even more important than they actually are. One aspiring bureaucrat brought his own carpet from home to put in his office. He also brought in a name plaque, which he very carefully mounted on his door. The senior executives in another department all brought radios with them. When I arrived to interview one of them, the gentleman in question was sitting there with a perfectly clean desk (except for the morning paper), listening to the radio. In fact, the office of one of the most senior officials in this department was so elaborate that it proved somewhat embarrassing. When I arrived at his office for a consulta-

tion, his senior secretary (ensconced in her office) told me to enter, because the gentleman was waiting for me. I opened the door, entered the inner sanctum; and closed the door behind me.

When I did not see our superior at his desk, I began to look around. I knew he must be somewhere, because his secretary had not seen him leave, and his radio was still on. I was about to look behind the sofa when suddenly I heard the unmistakable rush of a toilet flushing. Part of the mahogany-panelled wall opened and out stepped my lost superior, zipping up his fly.

Occasionally, through error, someone is given better furniture than his salary calls for. This, I am sad to say, happened to me once; I discovered that such situations are soon rectified. When I arrived for work one day and went into my office, one of the clerks asked me if I noticed anything different. When I didn't, she pointed out that my desk had been exchanged for a smaller one. It turned out that I had originally inherited a director's desk. When the mistake was recognized, movers were sent to my office, where they removed everything from the desk, put a smaller one in its place, and left. A short time later a new director was appointed who wanted a bookcase. It was then discovered that I was in possession of one illegally (that is, I had furniture above my station). Again, the movers were sent; they removed all my books and left.

There are times when the furniture hierarchy can be used to kick people when they are down. Take the case of one Acting Director who was in political disfavour and was in the process of being demoted. A demotion never results in lower salary, but rather fewer duties and, when possible, public humiliation – similar to the militaristic ripping off of epaulets. In this department there had been another re-organization and a Director General had been appointed. (When the governments re-organize, it often results in the creation of more senior executive posts.) This new Director General did not have furniture commensurate with his status. His former office was now filled by his replacement, and his Director General's office was bare. New furniture was ordered, but in the meantime this man needed something upon which to rest both his seat and his elbows. At this point he remembered the poor, disfavoured Acting Director and movers were dispatched forthwith. As the movers cleared the papers off the top of his desk and emptied his desk drawers, they kindly informed him that the Director General needed the desk and chair that they were so promptly and efficiently removing.

In another department senior people take all their furniture with them when transferred to another position within the same organization. Fear of the possibility that they may not receive furniture commenserate with their status and comparable to what they already have results in their covering themselves in this way. The CYA principle keeps a lot of movers busy.

My investigations have revealed that the preoccupation with furnishings and office space can seriously interfere with the course of important government business. One re-organization resulted in Harry being removed from his position and sent to another section. Harry, of course, took his furniture with him, leaving his office vacant. This office remained vacant for quite some time. So George, an employee in that section; decided to move into it, since his own office was hot and stuffy and had no windows.

A few weeks went by before more changes were announced in the re-organization. Bruce's managerial job was swallowed up by Herman's new job, but something had to be found for Bruce to do in order to justify his salary. Therefore it was decided to give him Harry's old job. It turned out that Bruce had a nicer office than Herman, who was replacing him. Consequently Herman told Bruce he was taking his office. Bruce went off in search of a place to move to and stumbled upon George, who was occupying Harry's office. Since this office was bigger and brighter than all the rest and since Bruce outranked George, our upstart was ordered out. Of course, George agreed to move, since he had little choice in the matter. He did not know when this move was going to take place, because it depended on when the movers arrived to move Herman into Bruce's office, and then move Bruce into George's office.

Three days later George received a phone call from the Minister's office concerning a problem that had to be solved immediately. While he was discussing the issues on the phone, a couple of moving men stuck their heads in his door, smiled, and pointed at the furniture. George acknowledged their smile; whereupon one gentleman picked up George's coat rack and left, while the other removed each of his two side chairs. Somewhat flabbergasted, George looked up a moment later to discover both movers eyeing his desk rather covetously. While continuing his conversation,

George yanked the wall plug on his dictaphone just as the desk was lifted and whisked away. Presently, the friendly movers returned and pointed at George's credenza, which contained his files and upon which rested his telephone. Quickly, George transferred the phone to his lap and watched the last piece of furniture (save the chair he was sitting on) move out.

Unfortunately, the Minister was not able to get George's full concentration on the problem. Having your furniture moved out from under you and being left sitting on a chair in an empty office with the phone perched on your lap is not conducive to top-notch decision-making. The policy decision made that day turned out to be disastrous, and the Minister in question is no longer.

In my research into this aspect of the civil service I became interested in the possibility of the moving game breaking down. In the above example, chaos could have resulted if all the moves had not been perfectly orchestrated. What if work orders were issued only for Herman's move into Bruce's office and George's move back to his own office? If that had happened, Herman and Bruce would both have been in the same office with two sets of furniture. The movers would not have been

able to move Bruce out, since the invoice and work order were not ready. Fortunately, this move was so well planned that all the work orders were in perfect sequence and the move went off without a hitch.

In order to determine if the moving procedure does break down and with what consequences, I visited numerous departments and discreetly questioned scores of people. Much to my surprise, I was only able to find one example of two people accidentally ending up in the same office. This, however, was not a problem of moving logistics so much as one of lack of communication. When it comes to moving furniture, the system is so well oiled that mistakes are impossible to find.

In the one case I was able to isolate where two people shared one office and, in fact, the manager-ship of the same section, Lester became seriously ill and was off work for some time. It was decided to replace him as manager and Michael was given the promotion. No one had bothered to tell Lester that he was no longer in charge of this section and, after about six months, Lester decided to return to work; but also didn't tell anyone. Michael arrived for work bright and early one Monday morning only to be greeted by Lester, who was seated behind his old desk reading the morning paper and sipping his coffee.

Lester thanked Michael for looking after matters during his illness and asked Michael what he would be doing now. Michael informed Lester that he was continuing in his job and suggested that Lester should report to the boss for re-assignment. Both men refused to step down, or leave, or make inquiries; they both sat there and glared at each other.

Fortunately, there was a senior management meeting every Monday – otherwise both men would have sat there forever. Instead, both men went off to the meeting as the manager of the section. No one seemed to find this strange. People simply greeted Lester upon his return and inquired after his health. Michael pointed out the problem to his immediate superior, who was very sympathetic and who offered to consider it carefully, because it was a very complex problem. At that moment, the Assistant Deputy Minister came along and Michael explained the problem to him. Being an Assistant Deputy Minister, the man was able to grasp the full implications of this problem immediately and offered to solve it as quickly as possible. That afternoon, Lester was given a new assignment.

Once you've mastered the art of covering your ass with office furniture (metaphorically speaking), as a successful bureaucrat you must concern yourself with the proper demeanour for one newly ensconced in the appropriate office. Which brings us to the cult of the harried executive – the only kind of executive that there is in the civil service.

# 4

# The Harried Executive

Looking busy and official is an essential function of a bureaucrat. When I first started my career in the government, I was quite impressed by the feverish activities of my colleagues. I would sit there and watch them stride down the corridor with purposeful expressions on their faces. Often their desks would be buried in files and papers; empty coffee cups and cigarette butts would abound. I was impressed. That is, I was impressed until I tried to put my observations together. I noted things like feverish activity, agitation, hypertension, and protestations about how busy people were, all suggesting industrious productivity. Then I noted a complete lack of any output. Strange, I thought.

The next thing I noticed was the fact that I had very little work to do and yet my responsibilities were about equal with those of my colleagues. Gradually the light dawned on me: in the government, the function of the individual is not to attain a goal (the completion of a job); rather, the ultimate function is in the doing.

Now, to the rational, goal-oriented person, these two concepts are connected. We have a particular goal to achieve, a job to complete. We therefore sit down and figure out what work has

*Sure Fire Promotion Material...*

to be done to bring about this goal. But this is not how it usually works in the government. Most of the time the goal is forgotten and bureaucrats do busy work to keep them out of trouble and to help make the day pass quickly. At all costs, one must not let it be known that one has nothing to do; for if you were given real responsibility, you might no longer be able to cover your ass.

If you complete your job and don't have many other jobs to do anyway, all you can do is sit around. This would not be covering your ass, since a superior might ask why you are just sitting and make up something for you to do. As a result, our civil servants go to a great deal of trouble to appear busy. They take their time completing tasks, they complicate tasks so that they will take longer, they spread files about to give the appearance of industry, and they continually invent new diversions to give an industrious appearance.

Skeptics among you may not really believe me, so let me give you some of my observations from over the years. Recently, as a private citizen for whom the bureaucracy is supposed to work, I called a government department and requested that a particular form be sent to me. A week later I called again and requested that this form be sent to me. A week later I phoned again and demanded to know why I had not received the form. It was explained to me by an exasperated voice at the other end of the line that two weeks was not an unreasonable amount of time for me to wait. "After all," the voice said, "it is not just a simple matter of putting a form in an envelope and sending it to you. We get a lot of people phoning in asking for forms." (I wasn't surprised, since that was the sole function of this department.)

I don't know how their process worked, but I can tell you that the way it *should* work is not the way it did. The people answering phones should have a supply of all the forms that are sent out and a supply of envelopes. When someone calls in for forms the name and address could be written directly on the envelope. The appropriate type and number of forms could be shoved into the envelope and placed in an OUT basket. A few times a day a messenger could come around, pick up the envelopes, and take them to the mail room, where they are stamped and shipped out.

Simple! Well, not really. First, we have clerks whose jobs are classified as Information Clerks. They answer the telephone and take down the relevant information. This information is recorded on a form – probably called a "Requisition for Form Form – 76/001." The form had to be designed by forms analysts and printed in the print shop. Periodically, it has to be revised and improved upon.

Next, the Requisition for Form Form – 76/001 is sent to the supply room. Here, supply clerks process each form individually, initial the form, and send it to the file room, where it is filed by the file clerk. The stuffed envelope is then sent to the mail room. (In case you are wondering, I did finally get my form, after I resorted to calling the manager, the one he sent me arrived the same day (seventeen days after my first call) as the one from my original request. However, after a seventeen-day wait, the government workers had sent the wrong form anyway.)

As a new employee of a government department, you may find yourself making a few enemies with naive questions and attempts to complete work as quickly as possible. Never forget that the end is often forgotten because of the preoccupation with the means. You will frequently work with people like George, a colleague of mine who was in charge of a program that was costing the taxpayers a small fortune every year. Aside from the monetary cost, the program required considerable

effort on the part of many people right across the country. Despite this large cost and great effort, the program is about four years behind schedule.

At a meeting one day I asked George what the purpose of this program was. George hemmed and hawed, but basically was unable to answer the question. It seems reasonable that if you are going to request that people across the nation fill out a form which will take time, as this program did; if you are going to have specialists design the forms; if you are going to have other specialists travel across the country explaining the forms; if you are going to have other highly skilled, highly paid people figuring out how the information gathered should be processed; and someone to interpret the information and printers to print it, should you not know why you are doing all this?

You will always make waves if you do work that you are not supposed to do. One eager soul possessed some knowledge that was not essential to his job description and that impinged on the functions of two other job classifications. In his zeal to complete a publication, he utilized his special knowledge, spent a total of five minutes doing the work, and got his publication out. He was such a naive dolt that he really expected brownie points and a pat on the head. The pat on the head became a clout on the ear.

The proper procedure that he should have followed would have taken weeks. He should have written a memo to the systems department so that his request for resources could have been evaluated in light of the existing workload and been assigned a priority. The person finally assigned to do the work would have met with the memo-writer to determine his exact needs. Once this chosen person had completed the job successfully, it would have been turned over to another department, which would have taken the work done by the systems people and set it up for printing. A memo would have been required from Memo-Writer to the head of that section to arrange priorities and schedules. The procedure might have taken months to complete.

Not only do entire programs and departments expand in complexity to give the impression of being busy, but individuals employ all sorts of little tricks to create this same impression. Memo writing and committee work are so central to this effort that they wlll be dealt with in separate chapters; here we will touch on telephone calls and punctuality.

Only the most naive executive would be foolish enough to take his phone calls immediately. He very obviously can't be either busy or important if you can get through to him on the first call! Usually what you will get instead is one of these stock phrases:

1. "I'm sorry, Mr. Smith is at a meeting right now. May I have him call you?"

2. "I'm sorry, Mr. Smith is out of town and won't be back until Monday."

3. "I'm sorry, Mr. Smith just stepped out for lunch (coffee)."

So you leave your name and number and expect the call to be returned within a reasonable amount of time. Maybe, if you are lucky, two weeks later the mysterious Mr. Smith will call to explain that he has just been able to get to your message.

"Very busy, you know. What with meetings and field visits, I hardly have a chance to sit down. Look, I've only got a minute now, so what can I do for you?"

By this time you can't remember why you called him in the first place.

If you are unlucky enough to be a harried

executive actually caught within the confines of your office when the phone rings, do go through this little ritual, at all costs – just so that your caller does not get the impression that you are a nobody! The ritual goes like this:

"Good morning, Mr. Crat's office."
"Mr. Crat, please."
"Whom shall I say is calling?"
"Joe Smith."
"One moment, please." (Click; a long silence, punctuated by occasional static.)
"Joe, how are you? B.U. Crat here. What can I do for you today? Can't take much time with you, just got back to town from Baffinland. Quite a few problems up there that I had to look into and now I have to write a report on the whole thing for the Deputy by twelve. It's just go, go, go, all the time. Could you hang on for a moment? There's another call for me."

Another way to appear very important is never to be on time. After being in the government for awhile, one begins to realize how inadequate Canadian upbringing and education are. We are always taught the importance of being on time. What deception! The school system stressed a virtue called "punctuality", which was an indication of your politeness and responsibility. Being late in the government is a mark of importance; the later you are the more important you are. If you can be on time for an appointment, you obviously don't have much to do. Keeping people waiting also gives you power over them. If you have enough authority to make someone wait, you have established your power over him.

The procedure is to summon your colleagues for a meeting. Upon their arrival in your outer office, which, hopefully, houses two secretaries, the guests are told to have a seat; the boss will be with them shortly. The arrival is announced via intercom. A half hour later, the inner office door creaks open and the boss steps out.

"Oh, are you all here already?" one exclaims. "I'm sorry, I was tied up and I thought Harry hadn't got here yet. Do come in. Can I get you coffee?"

My grade five teacher would have severely reprimanded him but, as a bureaucrat, he got full marks. By keeping us waiting he reinforced the fact that he was in control and we were mere hirelings. He also let us know how busy he was, since he lost track of half an hour after being told of our arrival, simply by being wrapped up in his work.

If you think this explanation is far-fetched, let me give you an example. One Deputy Minister called a meeting with all the senior employees of a particular branch, including the Assistant Deputy Minister in charge of that branch. The meeting was scheduled for eleven o'clock and we all arrived at the appointed hour. As the boardroom chairs would not accommodate all those gathered, the workers carried chairs into the open space on the floor and waited for the meeting. And waited. And waited.

At about 11:45 the door to the Assistant Deputy's office opened, and who should emerge but both the Deputy and the Assistant Deputy. Both must have been in that office since before eleven because everyone else was present at eleven and there is only one entrance to that office, which adjoins the boardroom. I guess they felt that they had to sit in there and chat, because it would not look good for them to be on time. While they sat and chatted, everyone else sat and fumed.

Since the man who kept us waiting was a Deputy Minister, he felt no compulsion to apologize or to explain why he was late. He arrived, sat down, and began. If anyone is owed an explanation it is the poor taxpayer; for no one sitting there twiddling thumbs till the meeting began earned less than $15,000 a year; the average was probably closer to $20,000.

The director that I worked for was a protege of this Deputy and was a sheer genius at playing the harried executive. He regularly showed up late for his own meetings and would then rush off early, because he had another meeting to attend. Once he arrived half an hour late for one of his meetings, only to discover that it had been cancelled when those of us who had arrived on time got fed up and left. Which goes to show you that sometimes you can go a little too far in covering your ass.

# 5

# The Paper Explosion

Two inventions, the photocopy machine and the portable dictaphone, have enabled government bureaucracies to expand at a phenomenal rate. Now one typist can produce enough copies of a memo to paper walls or to make her boss seem very, very important. While she is busy at the photocopy machine, her erudite superior, armed with his pocket dicta, can be composing, wherever he is - bathroom, bus, car, bed - anywhere!

In the government, getting and sending memos and letters is a mark of acceptance, the way the valentine is to a child. Remember back in public school when we sent out valentines in our class? Remember how upset you were when, out of a class of thirty, you only received two cards? Civil servants are no different. Acceptance and importance are measured by paper. Here are the rules of the game and the associated logic:

1. The more memos you send, the more important you are.

2. The more memos you get, the more important you are.

3. If you send a memo to someone, he will have to reply by memo.

4. Therefore, the more memos you send, the more memos you will get.

5. The more memos you get in reply, the more memos you will have to answer.

6. When you send a memo, get a reply, and answer, you will need to set up a filing system so that when you get a reply you can match it with your original memo so that when you reply to the reply you can refer to what you said in your first memo so that you do not contradict yourself. (That is, cover your ass.)

7. With all these memos being typed, mail being received, and files being set up, you will need your own secretary (or two). This means that you are very important. You will also have a lot of files. This means you will need a lot of filing cabinets, which looks very impressive.

As you go from point one to point seven, the logic becomes somewhat more complex. Nonetheless, even government messengers understand all the reasoning. I can recall one befuddled messenger who not only brought the mail but also the pay cheques. Because this particular department lacked any class whatsoever, the cheques were not in envelopes and the messenger knew everyone's take-home pay. This poor lad was always terribly confused when he reached my office, for he would mumble, "You sure make a lot of money for someone who doesn't get much mail."

This poor chap's attitude was not surprising, since this department was the most prolific that I had ever seen – although I did hear of another department where they were forced to take over part of an underground parking garage to store all their files; but I was never able to verify that. I did see, first hand, the feverish activity of Barry, my Director. This man was such a genius that he kept two secretaries going full time. The mail that came in and out of that office was a veritable flood of paper. I wondered when the man had time to write or compose all this, until one of his secretaries told me that she had refused to type any more memos that were dictated in his car. The car engine noise in the background gave her a headache. (She didn't mention whether the sound of tearing bathroom tissue could be heard on the tape as well.)

What were all those missives about? An example is presented for your information:

Memo to:    All Directors, Department "X"

From:       Barry Terry,
                  Director of Proliferation

Re:         Lunch Meeting

As you may recall, it was agreed at the last lunch meeting that I would arrange our next luncheon date. After informal discussions with a number of you over the past ten days, there appeared to be a consensus that MacDonald's would be the best location. My secretary has checked with the manager and has informed me that they were able to accommodate us.

I propose that this meeting take place at 1:00 p.m. on Tuesday, the 12th day of January. Since my schedule is quite crowded, as I am sure all of yours are as well, I would appreciate it if you would let my secretary know your order by the eleventh. If I can notify the management of our wishes on the morning of the meeting, it will facilitate our entry and exit and leave more time for our discussion.

The details above are fabricated, but the subject is not. Such a memo would result in replies from those who could not make the lunch date. This would cause Barry Terry to send out another memo, changing the date of the lunch; and it could go on forever.

Barry Terry had a lieutenant who strove very hard to emulate his director. Lewis the lieutenant was the epitome of a career civil servant. The section that Lewis was in charge of was housed in an open-space area, a new design feature of some office buildings, where there are no private offices but rather spaces divided by plants, dividers, and bookshelves. Lewis sat at a desk beside a five-foot-high divider; on the opposite side sat one of his employees, a man called Ken. When Lewis wished to pass information or instructions to Ken, he would dictate a memo to him. Both Ken and the secretary could hear every word that was being said. Why Ken never got up, looked over the divider, and answered the memo just as it was being dictated, I will never know. It never dawned on Lewis to dispense with the memo, lean over the divider himself; and say, "Hey Ken, how about . . . ." If Lewis stopped writing his memos he might have had nothing to do.

Like his boss, Lewis pretended that he was important by dictating memos in the strangest places. He returned to work from a trip one day with a sad tale of woe. It seems that during the plane trip he was sitting too near the engines, so he had to talk loudly into his portable dicta in order to be intelligible over the sound of the engine. For some reason his seatmate didn't take too kindly to this activity and made some suggestions as to what Lewis could do with his dictaphone. Lewis didn't elaborate on the suggestion, but he did complain that he was unable to get his memos written.

One day I had an opportunity to sit and watch Lewis actually *write* an important memo. The man was already known far and wide for written instructions to clerks which contained choice phrases like "Assimilate the two pages by means of a staple." How, then, did he write a memo? Paper-prolific Lewis probably spent more time on the memo that I saw him write than most short-story writers spend on one of their products. His fool-proof procedure provides a master plan for all who wish to cover their asses. The first step in writing his memo was to obtain all the files that would contain information on the given topic. He then carefully went through all the files, finding out what other people had said on the subject. Extensive notes were made, and then Lewis determined if the position he originally wanted to take was consis-tent with positions taken earlier by his superiors. If not, he would then adjust his thinking to bring it in line with what his research had indicated was existing policy.

Now that his position was set, he drafted the memo, which was then typed. The typed copy was just the first draft and had to undergo considerable revision. Contentious phrases were studied at great length, certain words were checked in a thesaurus to see if a better substitute could be found, and any word that might carry more than a neutral meaning was changed to its most vacuous synonym. If a technical word or two could be fitted in, that was done, even if Lewis did not fully understand their meaning, they sounded good. Finally, Lewis' memo was ready! He had probably changed its intent drastically from the original and he was as neutral as possible, but he had at least put a position on paper. He had also covered that important part of his anatomy.

When it comes to important things like taking a position; neutrality is very important. One department that frequently replied to requests for information from members of the public estab-lished the policy of signing all letters with "The Director, x Division." No name could be typed above this, because there was no director. The actual signature would be the employee's, followed by "for". No one could read the signature.

One civil servant in this department received a couple of replies to the letters that she had sent out, thanking her for the help she had given. Well, the letters weren't addressed to her. They were addressed to "The Director." The employee felt that she should be the one to whom the thanks and praise were directed, since she had done the work. She also felt that, given the fact that she was a professional, she should also be willing to take the responsibility if there was an error.

It turned out that no one could tell her why letters were signed with such anonymity. When she suggested to her bosses that this be changed, panic appeared in faces, dormant ulcers twitched, and blood pressures crept ever upward. Imagine! Someone was willing to admit that they were responsible for doing something. "We'll look into this," they said.

When no decision was forthcoming, she began signing letters with her own signature and title. The ensuing panic rivalled the combined chaos of *The Towering Inferno, The Poseiden Adventure,* and *King Kong.* The typing pool was ordered, in writing, not to type anything but the old signature. Memos were distributed advising all professionals who had occasion to write letters of the existing policy.

Files were studied to find confirmation of the policy. No confirmation could be found. The policy was not policy, but something that was carried on because everyone thought it was policy. A memo was drafted setting out the circumstances under which highly paid professionals could sign their own names and take responsibility for their work. The Maalox and Valium were put away until the next time a trouble-maker stirred the bureaucracy from its sleep.

In another case, a manager in charge of setting up a new program had a working committee doing the work; Project Manager reported to a steering committee that was supposed to oversee and "steer" his work. About a month after work began, the steering committee called the workers and their Manager together and severely chastised them for being derelict in some of their duties. They admitted that work was progressing well and on schedule, but they were upset because the group was not writing enough memos to keep the steering committee informed of our progress.

"How are we supposed to know what you are

doing?" they asked. Project Manager suggested that, since two of the members of the steering committee had offices within fifty feet of his and they usually had coffee together, they ask him. That, they felt, was not good enough.

"Look," they said, "what if you get hit by a truck on the way home and die. We won't know what you have done."

"But everyone on the committee has a certain job and getting it done on time is their responsibility," Project Manager replied. "If I get killed tonight they still know their jobs and will do them. In fact, they know what they are doing better than I do. All I do is co-ordinate."

"That doesn't matter. You have not written memos to us, so you have been negligent. From now on, write memos – or else."

So he wrote memos. In the government you win some and you lose some. The trick is to learn to roll with the punches. But always cover your ass by writing memos.

Another department established the policy that regional heads were supposed to send information to the central office on a special form every month. They always attached these forms to a memo, which read something like:

Enclosed herein please find forms 8 and 7 for the month of February for the Kichykoo Regional Office duly completed as per the instructions of the general manager dated 21/2/68.

Not only did these bureaucrats send a covering memo for the memo, but they sent an extra copy as well. There is no limit beyond which the CYA principle cannot be taken.

**6**

# The Committee: *Where Schizophrenia Abounds*

The existence of committees and task forces in the government serves two functions. First, they create work and give people a sense of self-importance. Second, they are an intangible creation – unlike one's own derrière – that can be blamed for failure or foul-up.

The first thing a bureaucrat thinks of when a problem arises is setting up a committee to do the work. Work has to be done, but who has time to be on a committee? The powers that be set up a working committee composed of four or five people, with one person as the chairman. The chairman does not necessarily have to know anything about what is to be done, and usually he doesn't. His job is to call meetings, which requires quite a bit of work. It is not easy to find one time and place that is agreeable to all members. He must then chair the meetings and solicit views from those present. If work is to be assigned, he must find someone to assign it and to get an estimate of the time required to complete it. Most important of all, the chairman must either take the minutes or assign this chore to someone else. Progress reports are to be written and typed. The chairman must then circulate the draft to the other committee people to ensure that he is accurately representing the

views of all concerned. Once this is done, the progress report is sent up the line to the boss.

Of course, most people are often on more than one committee at a time, which means that they do have a lot of meetings to attend, minutes to take, coffee to drink, and drafts to read and correct. How quickly and how well the work gets done is another matter. Certainly going to all those committee meetings and subsequently getting and sending all those papers does tend to give you the appearance of being quite busy and important.

The phenomenon of the bureaucratic committee chairman makes a fascinating subject of study. The following story describes an archetypal chairman. A few years ago it was decided to do a national survey to determine the effect of a change in legislation that was being widely criticised. (No one had made any attempt to evaluate the impact of these changes before they were made.) The person assigned to head the committee had no experience or training in running national surveys. His previous experience was totally unrelated to this function. If I mention his occupation it may help to identify him, so suffice it to say that the minimum qualifications of his previous occupation are ten years of formal education and good moral character. The Assistant Chairman had held the same previous occupation.

Running a national survey requires considerable technical expertise and training, which neither of these gentlemen had. The Assistant Chairman was completely uninformed about anything technical. One day a committee member answered her telephone intercom to hear the voice of Assistant Chairman Bob. Bob informed her that he had received a call on the first telephone line by mistake and that he thought it might really be a question that she should handle.

She glanced at the phone lights and noticed that the light on line one was not flashing – indicating that it was not on hold.

"Is the party still on the phone, Bob?"
"Yes, he is. Can you take the call?"
"Wait a minute," she said. "How can you call me on the intercom if you don't have line number one on hold?"
"Oh," he said, "I just put my receiver down on the desk and ran down the hall to find another phone to call you on."
"Why did you do that? All you have to do is push the hold button, then push the intercom

button, and you can call me without cutting the person off."

"Is that how that works? I've never been able to figure it out."

This man was second in charge of a national study designed to evaluate the impact of government policy, the man in charge wasn't much better. I don't remember the exact cost of this exercise, but rest assured that the taxpayer paid well in excess of $100,000.

How valid were the results? After more than a year of work, the department that had originally requested this project took everything that had been done up to that time and hired a team of outside consultants to finish the job. The chief consultant who was assigned this nearly impossible task had to work closely with the Chairman and Assistant Chairman. To mention their names to this consultant sets off a Pavlovian reaction of grinding teeth, snarled lip, narrowed eyes, and increased respiration, heartbeat, and blood pressure. And what of the Chairman? He has been promoted and assigned more important work.

Anonymity is extremely important for task forces or policy committees – groups set up to examine existing policy and to recommend changes. What's more, through the process of evolution, senior civil servants, who usually dominate such committees, have reverted to the invertebrate stage. Their spines have atrophied from lack of use. (See Chapter Nine for an explanation of this phenomenon.) As a result of this physiological defect, they always travel in packs or herds for protection. These characteristics are prerequisites for task-force or policy-committee membership. All reports are in the name of everyone on the task force, so should anything be even the slightest bit controversial, no one person can be singled out and blamed.

A few years ago I was asked by my Director to prepare a position paper on a certain problem for a task force being run by another department. Despite the almost impossible nature of this assignment as a result of there being almost no reliable information, I was ordered to do the study. After considerable work, utilizing the only information available, I wrote my report. The information that I did have was published by a third government department and could be obtained by anyone upon request. My report concluded that what was believed to be a problem was not. My name appeared on the document because I had done the work.

The Assistant Deputy Minister studied this document for quite some time and finally recommended two changes. First, my name was to be removed. Second, the document was to be classified as *confidential*. My name was removed because the position that the department took was that all policy papers be anonymous, presumably so that no one person or group of people could be blamed. It was probably classified because the position taken was somewhat controversial, since I had shown that there really was no problem at a time that the public was convinced that there really was one. The scramble to find a "confidential" stamp and the search for previously distributed copies was mildly amusing.

The findings of this particular paper could have alleviated a great deal of speculation in the press that went on for over a year, and it would have saved a group of people considerable embarrassment. Nonetheless, the findings were never released voluntarily and were only given out when word got out about the existence of the study, which was about a year after the study was produced. I will assume that with all the paper that flows back and forth in the government, this particular set of pages was forgotten about.

From these examples it is evident that committees are rather cumbersome creations headed by incompetents. But how and why are such people selected to head a committee? Of the many case histories with which I was supplied, the following story best illustrates the pattern and the rationale.

A particular department was given the problem of analysing the causes of increasing expenditures in a program designed to help a certain segment of the population. The senior person who was given the task was, as usual, totally unqualified for the job. He gathered about him some other people who were able to do the work and to provide him with considerable information. These people eagerly set to work and in a short time they came up with some novel findings. These indicated that a certain group of people and certain companies were abusing this program, at a substantial expense.

The task leader was given the findings. He reacted with the expected horror. The group that was identified as keeping costs up was politically powerful. How can we attack them? Instead, the

**An Expert...**

task leader was convinced that another group that was politically weak was abusing the system and he ignored the findings.

The honest investigators mentioned their findings to the task leader's superior, but he chose to ignore their comments as well. After all, Task Leader was in charge. A few weeks went by. Task Leader called a meeting to announce a discovery that proved that his politically weak group was abusing the system; he wanted confirmation from the experts. The experts, however, quickly showed that this evidence was incorrect and misleading and that the politically weak group not only accounted for a very small proportion of total expenditures, but could not be proven to be abusing the program. All was dropped.

What emerges is this: if the person most capable of analyzing the problem had been given the task, he would have come up with a very embarrassing report, which would have upset the upper echelons of the ministry. Instead, the experts were relegated to a secondary role under the direction of our incompetent. This tactic served two very useful purposes. First, the task leader would not be capable of coming up with anything original, controversial, unique, or potentially embarrassing.

If something like that did come out of the work of his committee members he would probably not be able to understand it. Second, even if he could understand it and agreed with it, he would not take a stand. Being incompetent and unqualified for one's job results in insecurity and reluctance to take a stand on any issue. Our experts were strong in their claims and kept pressing the point, simply because they had enough knowledge to back up their arguments with considerable strength. Unless they mend their ways, they will never head a committee!

The use of the fear of passing on controversial findings as a reason for appointing unqualified people to head committees is well illustrated by a report from another department. In this particular department the person given responsibility for projecting expenditures for a particular program was, again, totally unqualified for this chore. He gathered experts about him who were familiar with the standard chores that have been developed over the years for performing this very difficult task. These experts concerned themselves only with an honest appraisal of facts, an analysis of past trends, and an evaluation of future events. Their estimate of the next years' expenditures was rejected by the

...& Another.

REPORT

committee head – they had projected a greater increase than the Minister wanted to admit to.

It seems that the Minister had ruled that next year expenditures would be held to the maximum 7 per cent increase, no matter what. Therefore the committee head had to come up with an estimate that was within the maximum limit set in the guidelines by the politicians. The fact that this increase was not based on real need did not matter; the Minister had to be told what he wanted to hear. The unqualified committee head could reject the honest evaluation because he was unfamiliar with the standard techniques that were used and did not understand them. Being insecure in his position, he would not dare to tell the emperor that his ass was uncovered.

I would like to conclude this chapter with a little story about Jack and his many hats. The way this true story was told to me, Jack was a member of a committee who was assigned the task of writing a memo from the committee to the Minister of his department. The Minister read the memo and felt obligated to reply. But Ministers usually only *sign* their memos and letters; they do not *write* them, since they are not terribly familiar with what their departments do. So Jack, as an employee of the department, was assigned the job of replying to the memo that he himself had just written. A psychiatrist might call that schizophrenia. But for a civil servant, it is just another typical working day.

# 7

# The Joys of Empire Building

Somewhere in the offices of our nation's capital there is a ping-pong table. It is there because all of the employees of the section chipped in and bought it. They did it because they were bored – they have nothing else to do. Their section has been in existence for two years, but no one knows why. No one knows what they are supposed to be doing. They are the product of the joys of empire building.

The purpose of building an empire is to give yourself a greater importance than is actually deserved and, as a consequence, more money. However, money is not as important as the power trip. There is an old joke in bureaucratic circles about the official who gladly accepted a pay cut in order to be called "Director".

Power tripping by building an empire requires that you increase the size of your staff, even though the amount of work in the department cannot justify this increase. Not only do you require more staff, but you require more highly qualified staff. The person in charge of fifteen clerks is simply a Supervisor of Clerks; but the person in charge of five clerks and three university-trained professionals is a Section Chief or maybe even an Assistant Director. Thus, their job descriptions must be

worded in such a way as to enable you to upgrade your own position.

In order to increase your staff you must keep your present staff busy and you yourself must appear to be busy. As was pointed out earlier, memo and letter writing and committee meetings are designed for this end. Your staff is kept busy by increasing the complexity of their jobs rather than by streamlining the work flow. (Don't forget that a camel is a horse designed by a committee.)

In the course of my research I discovered a division that was trying to build the most incredible empire I have ever encountered. The Director and his Assistant decided that the entire staff was terribly overworked. (There was so much work that most people were forced to take long lunches and read two newspapers a day so that boredom didn't overwhelm them). In order to prove their point and increase their staff, these fearless leaders came up with this little scheme. Every request for work or for information that this division obtained had to be assigned a project number and had to be sent to the departmental senior management committee for approval. Everything had to be done in writing.

In order to show that this scheme works and how, here is an actual case history of one "project".

1. An elected member of the legislature asked a question of another department, called "A."

2. That department could not answer the question and thought that this empire-building department "B" would have the answer.

3. An Assistant Deputy Minister in department A called the Assistant Director of department B for the answer.

4. He informed department A that department B required this request in writing and that it would probably take about two weeks to service.

5. The Assistant Director of B checked his book of project numbers and assigned a number to it.

6. An information officer was summoned and informed that a letter was to be received shortly; requesting certain information, and he was given the project number.

7. The information officer wrote a memo to the Director requesting permission to act on this request and outlining the time needed to do the job.

8. The memo was then sent to the Director General, who took it to the next meeting of the senior management committee.

9. The Assistant Director wrote a memo to the Director General, pointing out that we were overworked and if we set a precedent by answering a request from an elected official, this might result in a deluge of requests.

10. The senior management committee met and deliberated and brought in their ruling. We must answer this request and any other we get from the legislature.

11. The information needed to answer the request had to be retrieved by another section. Therefore, the information officer had to write a memo to the director in charge of this section.

12. He read the memo, decided who was least busy, and told that person to do the work.

13. Finally, the information officer got the information, wrote a memo, and sent it off – about four weeks after the initial request from the legislator.

The servicing of this request cost the taxpayers somewhere between $200 and $300. This "project" was assigned a number under one person's responsibility and, as long as it was uncompleted, indicated that he was busy. Based on this type of documentation, the division could successfully argue for more staff.

The concept of management is unknown in the government. Instead of managing, the government administers; each so-called manager is given a lump sum of money at the beginning of the fiscal year and he administers its spending. If he does not have all his money spent by the end of the year, his budget the following year is reduced by that amount. Most typewriter, calculator, and office-supply salesmen who deal with the government can attest to the fact that their business improves greatly in February and March, as government departments rush to dispose of excess funds by the March thirty-first deadline. No one is ever awarded brownie points for underspending his budget rather than exceeding it. All budget submissions are devoted solely to justifying the need for expansion, never to improved efficiency.

A consultant was once approached by the managers of a particular government operation, given a pile of documents and numbers, and asked to justify one of their programs. These people invested $100,000 a year in this program and they wanted to prove that it was so effective that they needed more money to expand. These managers were so naive that they were unable to calculate the true cost. They knew that $100,000 per year was allocated for rental of special equipment and salary for special people needed to do this particular job. But they neglected to calculate the salary of their own regular staff who were allocated to assist in the project, or the cost of their own equipment, which was also used in the exercise. A more realistic cost figure would probably have been something like a quarter-million dollars per year. This program had been running for about eight years and a conservative estimate of the cost to the taxpayer over that time would be 1.5 million dollars.

A million and a half dollars of our money had been blown and not one person had ever bothered to ask if the money was well spent. When they finally did get around to looking at the program, it was only to provide justification for its expansion. The consultant's evaluation of the program suggested that it was completely useless. His colleague was horrified and shocked when he mentioned that he was going to inform the emperor that he had no clothes on.

"You can't do that," one of them said, attempting to justify the program. Despite the fact that his figures could not be considered by any expert in the field to be proof of the success of the program, he wrote a report justifying it. The managers now had ammunition with which to argue for more funds.

Other staff members recommended that this particular program be compared to other programs designed to achieve the same ends, in terms of both the success they had in achieving their stated goals and the cost per unit. The managers were not interested in doing this. Why should they? They had what they wanted - an argument for more money. Proof of the indispensability of your department because of its constantly increasing need for staff, equipment, and funds is the cardinal way to cover your ass. Besides, if you break the rules and economize, you will be blowing everyone else's cover - and consequently that of your precious posterior.

Through extensive interviewing I have been able to develop a generalized picture that illustrates the empire-building process. The following scenario is hypothetical, but the principles and growth pattern are accurate.

Department X discovers that there is some need to provide information to the members of the public who occasionally phone or drop in. Therefore they decide to set up an information-dissemination section under Theodore, who is given some office space and two clerks to perform the duties. Theodore is very ambitious and would like to be more than just a supervisor of two clerks. As we learned earlier, the way to do this is to increase the size of your staff and the complexity of their jobs, and to upgrade their qualifications.

Theodore begins by having his clerks fill out a form every time they disseminate information, either over the phone or on a face-to-face basis. The number of filled out forms grows substantially; consequently more space is required and someone must be hired to set up and maintain a proper filing system. By this time more office space is required, since we have so many forms and an extra clerk to sort and file them in many cabinets. Also, because the clerks are doing more than just passing out simple information (they are filling out forms), they have been upgraded. Theodore called in the job description people and had all the clerical people changed to Information Officers. In the process, of course, Theodore had to be promoted.

Sometimes, toward the end of a long day, practice being 'civil'— but don't let anyone catch you... least of all a member of the public or a superior...!

Now, because the clerks were more important, they could not have people simply wander in off the street and talk to them. Theodore had to hire aa receptionist, who screened calls and members of the public before they were eventually referred to the appropriate Information Officer.

The Information Officers had become quite busy by now. The demand from the public had *not* increased, but their work had. First, they were busy filling out forms everytime they did anything. Second, as Information Officers, they had to keep abreast of events in the community; this necessitated their reading at least one newspaper a day. Third, they had to hold meetings to discuss plans and problems. Fourth, they had to go on periodic government courses and training sessions to improve their qualifications and knowledge. As a result, the job of serving the public was not being done.

Theodore had a perfect argument for expanding his staff and hiring more Information Officers. As a direct result, more clerks had to be hired to scrutinize and file all the forms that were being filled out by the new Information Officers. More office space was required. Supervision was becoming a problem, so Theodore promoted one Information Officer to Chief Information Officer and hired a Records Management officer to supervise the files. In the process, Theodore was upgraded from Manager to Director.

Still, Theodore was not satisfied. Empire building is a hunger that can never be satisfied. His next idea was to produce a series of brochures detailing the activities of his department. The fact that there was no demand for this service didn't matter. The demand could be created. After much negotiation, writing of policy papers, and high-level meetings, Theodore sold his ideas and set up his new section. This, of course, resulted in hiring a publicity manager; professional writers, and layout artists to produce these pamphlets. Theodore was now a Director General.

Of course, I could go on, since Theodore did. But the point is made. We expanded from two clerks and a supervisor answering simple queries to a huge structure, without any increase in the actual workload or demand from the public. In biology, when a simple cell begins dividing and growing at an uncontrollable rate oblivious to its original function, it is called a cancer. In the government, it is simply empire building – one of the many ways of covering your ass.

8

on't do it. That's my advice to aspiring
bureaucrats. It isn't done. Really. Thirty
years of research have proven the fact.
People who are busy keeping their asses covered
find it, naturally, quite impossible. I know what
they say about the business world, the halls of
Academe, professional people, farmers' daughters.
But in the world of the bureaucrat, what can't be
done by memo, isn't. Government office parties are
a sure cure for insomnia; and affairs between civil
servants are limited to certain untoward attentions
to the posteriors of superiors by ambitious, eager
underlings – which hardly passes for the real thing.

There is no sex in the civil service. (The next
chapter may help to clarify this point.)

# Sex in the Civil Service

Only her Analyst knows for sure ... and he missed most of it!

# The Policy-Formulation Process: A Threat to One's Health

It is in the area of policy-making that civil servants deserve the most compassion and serious attention – and those considering a career in the civil service should take particular note of the ominous data contained in this chapter.

The strain of one's job is something that is very difficult for anyone to leave behind when heading home after a busy day, but particularly so for the policy-making bureaucrat. In one year, there are 8,760 hours. In one working year we put in 1,960 hours or 22.4 per cent of all the available time. There is a new branch of medicine known as Industrial Medicine, which is interested in the relationship between physical ailments, work pressure, and working conditions. Different occupations seem to produce different physical symptoms. It is fairly widely accepted that people employed as air traffic controllers, for instance, have a much higher incidence of ulcers, hypertension, and heart disease than the general population. Studies presently under way indicate that civil servants in policy-making positions suffer from two physical and/or psychological maladies to a greater degree than other occupational groups. The evidence thus far indicates that these problems can be traced back to the nature of the job.

*Occupational*
*Hazards #1*
*(See text)*

POLICY #74-326-783

*A Policy-Formulator...*

The first problem is proving to be quite fascinating to orthopaedic specialists and to those interested in evolution. Civil servants have long complained about back problems which, at first, were assumed to be caused by poor posture and poor design of chairs. When neither chiropractic manipulation nor improved working habits helped, extensive tests were conducted on a sample of civil servants. These tests indicated that there was a progressive softening and withering away of the spine from lack of use. Experts in evolution firmly believe that if civil servants intermarry and produce offspring who, in turn, become civil servants, we could have babies born without backbones in only two or three generations.

The other occupational problem area is sexual, and this is divided into two areas. The first type of sexual problem encountered by civil servants is impotency. The other problem is premature ejaculation. Both problems have undergone extensive evaluation by internists, urologists, and psychiatrists. The tentative conclusions that these people have arrived at are as follows. The fact that civil servants who help formulate policy have such a difficult time taking a firm stand carries over into their personal lives. Consequently, they have diffi-

culty taking a firm stand in sexual matters. Sometimes, against tremendous odds, civil servants do come up with something concrete. On these few occasions, they become so excited at this new turn of events that they can't handle it and leak the news prematurely to the press. Again, this carries over into their personal lives.

Now that you have seen what a tremendous toll policy-making has on the health and hence the happiness of your servants, I would like to outline a hypothetical model of how government bureaucracies formulate new policies.

In one part of the country some politicians noted that more and more people were passing away. Actually, what happened was that a Cabinet Minister from a rural area noticed that a number of his most ardent supporters and campaign contributors had died between elections. These people were long-time residents of his constituency and he was naturally concerned. He was even more concerned when he discovered that their farms were being bought by young professional sophisticates from the city, who were fleeing the effects of urban sprawl. Sitting in the legislature bar one day, he mentioned his concern to a colleague who had also noted a similar trend in his constituency.

Upon asking around, it turned out that this phenomenon was quite widespread. Therefore the Minister of Health directed a pointed question at his policy advisors: "Why are so many people dying?"

His personal policy advisors were unable to answer this question, so a strongly worded memo gs sent to the Deputy Minister. The Deputy ordered the policy analysis section to conduct a full-fledged investigation into the causes of death in the province.

A task force was immediately set up to formulate plans. The first job of the task force was to elicit submissions from as many interested parties as possible. Since this was a confidential inquiry, the task force was not able to publicize its existence or to hold public meetings. Various people in the ministry presented their thoughts on the matter, but consensus could not be arrived at.

The research branch suggested that a team of consultants be hired to conduct an empirical study of the problem. This was agreed to and bids were solicited from private consulting firms and university researchers. Twenty research proposals were received, outlining the method of conducting such a study, the names and academic qualifications of the prospective investigators, the cost of doing the study, and the time required to complete it.

Between the time the question was first posed, and the time all the bids were received, six months had elapsed. A further three months were spent reading, evaluating, and discussing the various bids. Finally, Dr. George Harvey at the Institute of Death, Dying, and Terminal Diseases was chosen to do the study.

Dr. Harvey and his associates were able to promise that they could do an analysis of the factors involved in the deaths of a 10 per cent sample of those who had passed away in the previous five years and come up with the findings in nine months. The cost would be only $75,000.

Eleven months after starting work, Dr. Harvey submitted his report to the research branch. He was only $12,000 over budget. The research people all studied the findings very carefully and held a number of meetings among themselves. Finally, they were able to grasp the full implications of this research. Within two months of receiving the report, they sent their recommendations to the task force.

The task force, six weeks later, sent their recommendations to the Minister. This memo was initialed by the Deputy Minister within two weeks and sent to the Minister, who rushed off to Cabinet with it.

Almost two years had elapsed since the time that government members began noticing that many of their ardent supporters were dying, but now the government had a solution that would benefit every citizen and save them money, as well. It was decided to emphasize the money-saving aspect of the plan only, since people were strongly criticizing the government for overspending.

The solution to the death problem: the systematic closing of hospitals. It seems that Dr. Harvey found a very strong relationship between hospitalization and death. Almost 90 per cent of the people who died in a given year did so in hospitals. He argued that since governments set safety standards for cars and enforced safe driving habits in order to reduce deaths, it should close hospitals, because hospitals caused deaths. After all, most people who die do so in hospitals.

All potential civil servants who remain dedicated to this career in spite of hazards to health and happiness should study the above policy-making model closely. If you cannot understand its logic or do not agree with its methodology, you have chosen the wrong career. This is the acid test; if you fail, you'll never be able to cover your ass.

The above story was hypothetical, but the process that was executed is typical of the way that policy positions are arrived at. One of my informants told me of a policy study on funding that revealed some startling facts. It seems that expenditures for a particular agency were escalating considerably. Upon investigation, it turned out that the number of people who required and obtained the services of this particular agency were declining. At the same time, both expenditures and staff were growing. Very strong suggestions were made to deal with this problem, but the report is sitting somewhere in someone's office, ignored.

However, please do not get the impression that all policy is designed to waste money and that all money-saving ideas are ignored. I did manage to find one department that was very budget-conscious. This department had a number of vehicles. The departmental policy was that, in order to save money, anyone travelling could only fly in exceptional circumstances and only with senior-management approval. Normally, all employees would have to take a government car.

If a senior member of the department had to visit a city 250 miles away, the air fare would be about $75 and the transit time would be one hour each way. The traveller could fly to his meeting in the morning and fly home afterwards that very same day. Total cost including fares to and from the airport would probably amount to $100.

This type of extravagance was frowned upon, since the senior-management people felt that airfare was very costly. Instead, a car had to be taken. This was considered to be much cheaper, since the capital expenditure for cost of the vehicle, the gasoline, and the wear and tear did not appear on an expense account.

The time to get to and from this distant city by car was increased from two hours for the round trip to ten hours. The employees would not be expected to drive all this time in one day. Thus, they set aside one day for travelling to their destination, and one day for returning. On those two days their productivity was lost, so if they earned $75 per day we can add another $150 to the cost of the trip. This, also, did not appear on the expense account and was not considered. Finally, they needed somewhere to stay for two nights and they had to eat, so we can add that cost as well. The policy of this department was designed to save money by eliminating costly air fare; as you can see, the hospital model is not that absurd.

Even if the quality of most government policy is low, the cost of producing it is high. As you can imagine, the cost of the manpower for all those committees is quite substantial. Just to get an idea, let us take a quick look at the cost involved in coming up with the policy to close hospitals.

The actual cost of the research project (and the government does contract out quite a bit of research) was $87,000. Prior to deciding on a research project, a task force was at work, resulting in a cost of $10,000. Considerable time was devoted by the research branch to reviewing research proposals, meeting with the researchers, and co-ordinating the project. They then studied the final report, wrote summaries, and discussed the findings. This amounted to an additional $15,000. The time of people at other levels (making representations to the task force, the Deputy Ministers' time, etc.) amounted to $5,000. Overhead came to about $10,000. Total cost, therefore, was a mere $127,000. Not too bad!

If one is rash enough to rock the boat by spending less than that kind of money on a project, or – horrors! – to protest too much, one will definitely make waves among one's free-spending colleagues. And making waves is the cardinal sin among devotees of CYA.

# 10

# Promotions: *The Don't Make Waves Syndrome*

few years ago Laurence Peter, the world-renowned hierarchologist, developed what has become known as the Peter Principle. According to this analyst of bureaucracies, people are promoted for competence until they reach their level of incompetence. A person may be a superb teacher who is able to communicate and relate to his pupils; since the teacher cannot be rewarded for excellence beyond a certain monetary level, he gets his reward by being promoted to an administrator, where the pay is greater. The teacher probably enjoys his work and does not want to administer, but he does want recognition and a bigger pay cheque. As a result, he accepts the promotion. He, of course, has no experience or training as an administrator, and probably also has little interest in it. He inevitably fouls up the job. That person has been promoted to his level of incompetence.

This theorem of Professor Peter is a brilliant observation of events in the world. Civil servants, in their Alice-in-Wonderland fashion, have added a number of twists to this principle.

In all my research in the civil service, I could not find evidence of anyone who had ever been promoted for competence. That is not to say that

there are not a lot of very competent people in the government. There are! Often, they are very disgruntled and disheartened. The competent employees are usually young, bright, university graduates ready to reform the world. Some may be a little too enthusiastic in their zeal to perform. Most are quite sane, rational, and dedicated – the type who should do an excellent job and should be promoted. Instead, these people become very discouraged and often retreat into a shell. They become disillusioned when they try to perform their duties and find that no one cares.

People often react quite differently when faced with this type of problem and civil servants are no exception. In some cases the people are able to leave and forego the monetary benefits. Those who are not able to leave but who are disillusioned often develop eccentric habits. The most bizarre eccentricity I was able to uncover involved a yo-yo player. This poor soul found life so unnerving that he kept a yo-yo in his office. When things got rough, he would close his door and play for a few minutes.

What, then, is the criterion for promotion and advancement in the civil service? The bureaucratic amendment to the Peter Principle is this:

If you are standing up to your chin in polluted water, you do not want someone around who will make waves.

Therefore you promote people based on their inability to make waves. If someone does make waves, you remove him. Many of the people already in senior positions are incompetent. Therefore they do not want someone competent under them because that new person will obviously show them up. He will make waves. They promote on the basis of the "don't make waves" principle – on the basis of incompetence.

Occasionally someone will make waves because he is too incompetent. There *are* limits. The extreme incompetent cannot be tolerated since his incompetence causes problems, and he will be promoted in order to get rid of him. This concept of not making waves is an extension of the CYA principle. By making waves either through excessive zeal or sheer stupidity, you bring attention to yourself, to others, and to problems. As a result, people will be out to silence you in order that they can continue to cover themselves. The person who survives best is the one who helps as many people as possible to continue to cover their asses by making as few waves as possible. Below are some actual case histories to illustrate this theory.

*Case One:* In Chapter Six, where we discussed committees, we met the gentleman who was in charge of determining the impact that a change in legislation had. He was quite unqualified to perform this work. He did not do a very competent job but was given a promotion and assigned more responsible work. He did not make waves, since he came up with nothing that could be embarrassing to anyone. Many asses remained covered as a result of his work.

*Case Two:* In this same department, there was an assistant who was inherited when a new supervisor arrived. The assistant was lazy, irresponsible, and unqualified. Theoretically, the position he held should have been filled by someone with a fair bit of technical expertise. This person had none. When the supervisor tried to find out why he had been given the job, he was told the following: he had been with the government for quite a number of years and had started as a Clerk; gradually, he managed to work himself up to Head Clerk, where he proved to be quite irresponsible and incompetent; as a result, he was promoted to get him out of the way.

*Case Three:* A certain man, who holds the position of Chief in an area that he has little expertise in, was hiring staff. At the interviews he asked a number of technical questions to determine the qualifications of the applicants. Two of the people interviewed were known to be highly competent in this field. The questions the interviewer asked revealed that he did not know what he was talking about. In one case the person interviewed was quite confused because the question asked did not make sense. In the other case, the person being interviewed had no choice but to give the right answer – which was the wrong one for the interviewer, since he himself was confused about the subject. Neither of these people got the job. I suspect that they knew too much and would have made waves.

*Case Four:* One chap whom I discovered in the course of my research has received a number of promotions in the last little while and holds a fairly senior, highly paid post in a very technical field. The man works very long hours and is so wrapped up in his job that his nerves are shot. He carries a little bottle of tranquillizers in his attaché case. He is also highly educated, holding a doctoral degree.

The degree is in a completely different discipline than the one in which he presently works. There are no similarities whatsoever between disciplines, so nothing he has learned has prepared him for his present job. That is why he works so hard and is such a nervous wreck. He doesn't know what he is doing. He has been promoted because he is incompetent and is incapable of coming up with anything that could be the least bit embarrassing. His bosses certainly understood how to make the CYA principle work for them.

# 11

# The CYA Principle & Public Relations or *How to Abuse a Citizen Without Really Trying*

*I*n theory, the various levels of government exist to provide a service to both you and I. They are our servants, paid by us and dedicated to helping us. But have you ever tried to get any service from them? It is difficult. Aside from the fact that very often the public must be ignored when civil servants are busy building empires, the main reason for this necessity to avoid providing service is that the civil servant must desperately try to keep his ass covered. Simple matters can be dealt with - once the proper forms are filled out - but if the problem is complex, the servant will probably have to take a position of some sort. By taking a position he exposes himself, because he might not be correct. He could be criticized - or even reprimanded.

In order to prevent this from happening, there are a few tactics that the successful civil servant must be familiar with. First, instructions and rules and regulations must be made so complex that the public is encouraged to give up their quest for service. The regulation cited in the dedication is a perfect example of this. I seriously doubt if the author of that regulation was able to understand what he had done. In a similar case, some technical experts were asked to evaluate certain changes in

legislation. In order to do this they obtained the booklet distributed to the public that explains the workings of the program established under the legislation. Three men with a combination of seven university degrees resulting from a total of twenty years of university study spent several days unravelling the mystery. How was the average citizen supposed to understand this program?

I became so intrigued by this phenomenon of written instructions that confuse and confound citizens that I gathered as many government documents and instruction pamphlets as I could. I began a systematic search through them to find the most absurd example possible. This task proved to be more arduous than I had ever imagined – and almost disastrous. Not only did I develop severe eye strain but I soon began imitating in my speech the written style I was reading. The two weeks in the sun prescribed by my doctor restored my sanity. I am now able to provide you with a classic example of government double-talk.

The adult citizens in the land are required to have an identity card. The department in charge of issuing these cards has published a very nice booklet with a drawing of a group of your average citizens on the cover. There are numerous cartoons throughout the booklet and the type is not only large, but also in two or three different colours. Let us suppose that a citizen loses his identity card and he wants to have it replaced. His first step is to call the department responsible for these cards and they mail him all the forms and the instruction booklet. Our citizen looks in the table of contents and finds:

> Section 7: What To Do If You Lose Your Card . . . 11

Turning to page eleven, he finds:

> Section 7: What To Do If You Lose Your Card
>
> You may find that your card has been stolen, lost, or misplaced. In this case, simply see STEP TWO and follow the instructions (*i.e.* (a), (b), or (c)) that apply to you.

The citizen then flips through the booklet and on page three he finds STEP TWO, which says:

> Refer to the appropriate section of this Guide which, depending on your status, describes the *primary* document you must send along with your application:

(a) if you are a citizen, refer to Section 3;

(b) if you are a landed immigrant, refer to Section 4;

(c) if you are neither a citizen nor a landed immigrant, refer to Section 5;

(d) if you have had a card but want to register a change of name or other information, turn to Section 6;

(e) if you have had a card but you need a new card, turn to Section 7.

That's it: our citizen needs a new card because his old one was lost. So he turns to Section 7, which says:

What To Do If You Lose Your Card

You may find that your card has been stolen, lost, or misplaced . . . .

According to this simple booklet, it is impossible to get a lost card replaced. You simply get referred from one section back to another and never bother the civil servant. You can see why my mind almost snapped doing this part of the research.

Some people, unfortunately, are very persistent. They might not be deterred by the confusion created by the booklet of instructions. Sometimes they bother the civil servants, so strategies have been developed to fob people off. One gentleman I discovered disagreed with an assessment of certain of his property that had been made by a particular government department. In this case the departmental employee happened to be a computer who, the gentleman felt, did not quite understand the complexity of the issue. He therefore objected.

The human employees of the department suggested that if he did not approve of the ruling, he could appeal. This meant that he would have to fill out a form in triplicate, explaining his reasons for disagreeing with the assessment. These forms had to be filled out within a specified period of time and sent by registered mail. At this stage, most people would have given up. Not only was this gentleman persistent, but his lawyer encouraged him as well by providing him with legal precedents, which the lawyer claimed validated his claim. He therefore filled out the forms in triplicate, registered them, and sent them off.

After a few weeks went by, the appeals office

Well Mr Jones ... What can we do for you today?

10:15 AM

sent the gentlemen a letter informing him that his objection had been received. They promised that they would look into the matter in due time, and that the Minister himself would rule on the validity of this person's claim. (They were telling him in fact that when they turned him down again and upheld the computer's decision, the decision would be made not by a mere civil servant but by the Minister; this tactic is designed to instill sufficient fear into citizens that they will go away.)

After a fairly lengthy period of time, the gentleman received a letter from the appeals office instructing him to phone. When he did so, the civil servant informed him that they were unable to understand his argument.

"I can see why you think you are entitled to the extra money," the civil servant said. "Your lawyer gave you that advice. But I don't understand the argument. I don't think it is valid." The civil servant went on to explain that he would be forced to deny the appeal. If he did that, it would automatically be passed on to another level, where, the gentleman was assured, the original denial would be upheld.

"Why don't you just drop your claim, since we will refuse it anyway?" reasoned the civil servant.

"Well, all right," said the gentleman, who was

somewhat taken aback by all this.

"Good! I'll mail the necessary forms to you to sign so that your appeal will be officially withdrawn."

A couple of days later our hapless citizen received the proper withdrawal forms (to be filled out in duplicate) by registered mail. As you can see, the civil servants were reluctant to take a stand and refuse the claim. That meant that they would have had to justify their position (even if it was done in the name of the Minister) leaving themselves open for criticism. Much better to discourage people initially and, if that doesn't work, to "con" them into retreating. That way your ass is covered.

Our story, however, does not end here. The gentleman began to realize that he was being taken, so he called his lawyer. The lawyer advised him not to withdraw his appeal and to force the department to make a decision. He sent the appeal office a registered letter advising them that he would not back down.

The bureaucrats let the gentleman stew for a couple of months before sending him a registered letter advising him that the Minister was turning down his claim. (Note that important mail is always registered. Even the government doesn't trust the

But Mr. Jones... Let's try to be reasonable about this...!

1:35 PM

post office with mail.) This time the citizen was given a reason for the rejection. The Minister referred to a certain section and sub-section of an act which, he claimed, invalidated the gentleman's argument. This was a very impressive tactic, but by now the gentleman was getting progressively angrier and was no longer intimidated by cheap tactics.

Instead of giving in as most people would have, our good gentleman went off to the library. There he obtained a copy of the act in question and began studying it very, very carefully. When he got to the section and sub-section that the Minister claimed disqualified his appeal, he made a startling discovery. The Minister had just given him a classic snow job.

The section and sub-section of the act that was supposed to nullify the claim bore no relationship to it at all. It referred to something entirely different. It would almost seem that this section was quoted at random to impress the gentleman. The bureaucrats really didn't expect anyone to call their bluff and go out and read the act.

Our gentleman friend was not amused and has taken his claim to the next highest level. At the time of writing, no decision has yet been reached. As you can see, these tactics are brilliantly conceived in order to quickly dispense with the public, confuse them, intimidate them, and snow them. Potential bureaucrats, take note.

Successful bureaucrats often employ a delaying tactic and, when the citizen gets uppity, buy him off. In an infamous case one Malcolm, as a result of certain circumstances, felt that he was entitled to certain government benefits; the office that he dealt with advised him verbally that such was the case. When he moved, they told him to go to another office and they would forward his file. Of course, the file was misplaced somewhere and the new government office insisted that Malcolm fill out a new claim. When Malcolm heard nothing, he went back to the government office, but his file had not turned up. To top things off, the person he had originally dealt with had left and that bureaucrat had neglected to have Malcolm fill out other essential forms. For that reason his claim had not been acted upon.

This new civil servant assured Malcolm that he did not qualify for benefits. Malcolm persisted in his claim and, when he mentioned that he would like a written statement from the office stating that he did not qualify and the reasons why he did not qualify, the public servant panicked. He explained to Malcolm that he no longer qualified for benefits because the time period within which to apply had elapsed. Malcolm explained that it had elapsed because his file was misplaced in transit, and that another official was negligent in forgetting to have necessary forms filled out, which delayed the claim. Also that he wanted the refusal in writing for his lawyer.

At this point the civil servant assured Malcolm that he would carefully review the claim, take it up with his superiors, and send Malcolm a report. A few weeks later, Malcolm received a cheque in the mail. On the very next day he received a notification from the departmental computer telling him that he no longer qualified for benefits and that he was being cut off.

The civil servants that Malcolm encountered remembered the golden rule: delay the public, confuse them, and if they get uppity you can give them a small token to appease them. In this case, Malcolm was bought off with one cheque for a small portion of the benefits that he should have received. Malcolm had already wasted months and was not willing to fight anymore, which is what any self-respecting public servant wants. Keep your ass nicely covered, even if you must abuse a citizen in the process.

These tactics, along with all of the others in the book, may sound difficult to master, but I can assure you that they work, and soon they are second nature. I did not make them up. You now know why I prefer to remain anonymous. People will not act naturally in my presence if they think that I am observing them and making notes. They may even become angry and make me run a gauntlet of my peers, all of whom will be swinging strands of red tape at my bare, exposed backside.

Cover Y

ur Ass!

# Glossary

### The CYA Principle
This term stands for "Cover Your Ass". A peculiar bureaucratic activity designed to protect one's position and status from attack by others.

### Re-organization
The only constant in the government! As soon as the organizational structure is decided upon, someone decides that it is not good enough and a re-organization is required. With this continual change, bureaucracies remain in a constant state of movement, and thus in a constant state of confusion.

### Minister
An elected member of the government who is appointed to the Cabinet and put in charge of a department. Usually, he is totally unfamiliar with the workings of his department (sometimes called a "ministry") and he only provides general policy guidelines. For example, the Minister of Finance.

### Deputy Minister
A full-time career civil servant who really runs the department. This position is similar to that of a company president.

## Assistant Deputy Minister

Another full-time career civil servant, responsible to the Deputy Minister and in charge of part of the department. The number of these positions within a particular department is a function of the size of the department. This position would be analogous to a vice-president.

## Director General

The next position down the line. This person would be in charge of a number of divisions (sections) that could be lumped together because of some common element (such as a shared coffee machine or washroom).

## Director

The person in charge of a division within the department or ministry, and who usually reports to a Director General.

## Chief (or Manager)

The bureaucrat in charge of one part of a division, who reports to the director.

## Special Assistant to the Deputy Minister

Usually a highly paid bureaucrat who has been stripped of power but who must be accommodated by the organization. This person usually performs three functions – he sharpens pencils; he reads all the daily papers; he collects his pay cheque.

## Special Advisor

Same as above.

## Executive Consultant

Same as Special Advisor.

## Political Exile

A state where those who are disliked are banished to. They are given no duties, and are ignored until their friends regain power. The ex-president of some country may be a political exile in Paris until restored by the next coup, but for a civil servant his country is an office in a back corridor.

In order to truly cover his ass, Bureaucrat X has not been willing to supply biographical information. However, for those of our readers who might feel uncomfortable without some author identification, we can attest to the following:

Bureaucrat X was born in 1928 as the youngest son of a Hamilton steelworker. He was schooled normally and, against all kinds of adversity, struggled to win a full scholarship at the University of Toronto. He graduated with first class honours in 194–, specializing in economics and political science. He completed his master's degree at the prestigious London School of Economics. As a result of a brilliant and relevant thesis on the econometric model of the barter system of trade among the Kikuyu of Central Africa, he was offered over a dozen positions with the Canadian federal government.

Bureaucrat X's first major responsibility as a civil servant involved him in streamlining the Canadian postal system. Since that time, he has spent over thirty years in a plethora of bureaucratic positions, and he is now working on the script of a feature-length film based on this book, to be produced by the National Film Board next year.

# The Author

David Shaw was born in London, England, on Christmas Day 1947. He immigrated to Canada with his parents in 1954. Since graduating from the Ontario College of Art in 1969, Mr. Shaw has worked primarily in the field of book design with several major Canadian publishing companies. Books he has illustrated include *Saturday Night at the Bagel Factory* (Don Bell, 1972); *Compulsive Cookery: A Guide to the Fine Art of Neurotic Gastronomy* (Maureen Bendick, 1973); and *The Wit & Wisdom of Bob Edwards* (Hugh Dempsey, 1976). At present, Mr. Shaw lives in Toronto with his wife, Candace, and Cocker Spaniel, Poppy, where he is president of his own book design and production company.

The above was supplied by the illustrator to occupy two pages left vacant after a segment of the original manuscript was expurgated by the publishers' lawyers.

# The Illustrator

*Designed & produced by*
David Shaw & Associates Ltd., Toronto

*Typesetting by*
Howarth & Smith Limited, Toronto

*Printed & bound by*
John Deyell Company, Lindsay